HIPPIAS MINOR

PLATO

Translated by
BENJAMIN JOWETT

INTRODUCTION

The Lesser Hippias may be compared with the earlier dialogues of Plato, in which the contrast of Socrates and the Sophists is most strongly exhibited. Hippias, like Protagoras and Gorgias, though civil, is vain and boastful: he knows all things; he can make anything, including his own clothes; he is a manufacturer of poems and declamations, and also of seal-rings, shoes, strigils; his girdle, which he has woven himself, is of a finer than Persian quality. He is a vainer, lighter nature than the two great Sophists (compare Protag.), but of the same character with them, and equally impatient of the short cut-and-thrust method of Socrates, whom he endeavours to draw into a long oration. At last, he gets tired of being defeated at every point by Socrates, and is with difficulty induced to proceed (compare

Thrasymachus, Protagoras, Callicles, and others, to whom the same reluctance is ascribed).

Hippias like Protagoras has common sense on his side, when he argues, citing passages of the Iliad in support of his view, that Homer intended Achilles to be the bravest, Odysseus the wisest of the Greeks. But he is easily overthrown by the superior dialectics of Socrates, who pretends to show that Achilles is not true to his word, and that no similar inconsistency is to be found in Odysseus. Hippias replies that Achilles unintentionally, but Odysseus intentionally, speaks falsehood. But is it better to do wrong intentionally or unintentionally? Socrates, relying on the analogy of the arts, maintains the former, Hippias the latter of the two alternatives...All this is quite conceived in the spirit of Plato, who is very far from making Socrates always argue on the side of truth. The over-reasoning on Homer, which is of course satirical, is also in the spirit of Plato. Poetry turned logic is even more ridiculous than 'rhetoric turned logic,' and equally fallacious. There were reasoners in ancient as well as in modern times, who could never receive the natural impression of Homer, or of any other book which they read. The argument of Socrates, in which he picks out the apparent inconsistencies and discrepancies in the speech and actions of Achilles, and the final paradox, 'that he who is true is also false,' remind us of the interpretation by Socrates of Simonides in the *Protagoras*, and of similar reasonings in the first book of the *Republic*. The discrepancies which Socrates discovers in the words of Achilles are perhaps as great as those discovered by some of the modern separatists of the Homeric poems...

At last, Socrates having caught Hippias in the toils of the voluntary and involuntary, is obliged to confess that he is wandering about in the same labyrinth; he makes the reflection on himself which others would make upon him (compare *Protagoras*). He does not wonder that he should be in a difficulty, but he wonders at Hippias, and he becomes sensible of the gravity of the situation, when ordinary men like himself can no longer go to the wise and be taught by them.

It may be remarked as bearing on the genuineness of this dialogue: (1) that the manners of the speakers are less subtle and refined than in the other dialogues of Plato; (2) that the sophistry of Socrates is more palpable and unblushing, and also more unmeaning; (3) that many turns of thought and style are found in it which appear also in the other dialogues:—whether resemblances of this kind tell in favour of or against the genuineness of an ancient writing, is an important question which will have to be answered differently in different cases. For that a writer may repeat himself is as true as that a forger may imitate; and Plato elsewhere, either of set purpose or from forgetfulness, is full of repetitions. The parallelisms of the Lesser Hippias, as already remarked, are not of the kind which necessarily imply that the dialogue is the work of a forger. The parallelisms of the Greater Hippias with the other dialogues, and the allusion to the Lesser (where Hippias sketches the programme of his next lecture, and invites Socrates to attend and bring any friends with him who may be competent judges), are more than suspicious:—they are of a very poor sort, such as we cannot suppose to have been due to Plato himself. The Greater Hippias more resembles the Euthydemus than any other dialogue; but is immeasurably inferior to it. The Lesser Hippias seems to have more merit than the Greater, and to be more Platonic in spirit. The character of Hippias is the same in both dialogues, but his vanity and boasting are even more exaggerated in the Greater Hippias. His art of memory is specially mentioned in both. He is an inferior type of the same species as Hippodamus of Miletus (Arist. Pol.). Some passages in which the Lesser Hippias may be advantageously compared with the undoubtedly genuine dialogues of Plato are the following:—Less. Hipp.: compare Republic (Socrates' cunning in argument): compare Laches (Socrates' feeling about arguments): compare Republic (Socrates not unthankful): compare Republic (Socrates dishonest in argument).

The Lesser Hippias, though inferior to the other dialogues, may be reasonably believed to have been written by Plato, on the ground (1) of considerable excellence; (2) of uniform tradition beginning with Aristotle and his school. That the dialogue falls below the standard of Plato's other works, or that he has attributed to Socrates an unmeaning paradox (perhaps with the view of showing that he could beat the Sophists at their own weapons; or that he could 'make the worse appear the better cause'; or merely as a dialectical experiment)—are not sufficient reasons for doubting the genuineness of the work.

HIPPIAS MINOR

PERSONS OF THE DIALOGUE:
Eudicus, Socrates, Hippias

EUDICUS: Why are you silent, Socrates, after the magnificent display which Hippias has been making? Why do you not either refute his words, if he seems to you to have been wrong in any point, or join with us in commending him? There is the more reason why you should speak, because we are now alone, and the audience is confined to those who may fairly claim to take part in a philosophical discussion.

SOCRATES: I should greatly like, Eudicus, to ask Hippias the meaning of what he was saying just now about Homer. I have heard your father, Apemantus, declare that the Iliad of Homer is a finer poem than the Odyssey in the same degree that Achilles was a better man than Odysseus; Odysseus, he would say, is the central figure of the one poem and Achilles of the other. Now, I should like to know, if Hippias has no objection to tell me, what he thinks about these two heroes, and which of them he maintains to be the better; he has already told us in the course of his exhibition many things of various kinds about Homer and divers other poets.

EUDICUS: I am sure that Hippias will be delighted to answer anything which you would like to ask; tell me, Hippias, if Socrates asks you a question, will you answer him?

HIPPIAS: Indeed, Eudicus, I should be strangely inconsistent if I refused to answer Socrates, when at each Olympic festival, as I went up from my house at Elis to the temple of Olympia, where all the Hellenes were assembled, I continually professed my willingness to perform any of the exhibitions which I had prepared, and to answer any questions which any one had to ask.

SOCRATES: Truly, Hippias, you are to be congratulated, if at every Olympic festival you have such an encouraging opinion of your own wisdom when you go up to the temple. I doubt whether any muscular hero would be so fearless and confident in offering his body to the combat at Olympia, as you are in offering your mind.

HIPPIAS: And with good reason, Socrates; for since the day when I first entered the lists at Olympia I have never found any man who was my superior in anything. (Compare Gorgias.)

SOCRATES: What an ornament, Hippias, will the reputation of your wisdom be to the city of Elis and to your parents! But to return: what say you of Odysseus and Achilles? Which is the better of the two? and in what particular does either surpass the other? For when you were exhibiting and there was company in the room, though I could not follow you, I did not like to ask what you meant, because a crowd of people were present, and I was afraid that the question might interrupt your exhibition. But now that there are not so many of us, and my friend Eudicus bids me ask, I wish you would tell me what you were saying about these two heroes, so that I may clearly understand; how did you distinguish them?

HIPPIAS: I shall have much pleasure, Socrates, in explaining to you more clearly than I could in public my views about these and also about other heroes. I say that Homer intended Achilles to be the bravest of the men who went to Troy, Nestor the wisest, and Odysseus the wiliest.

SOCRATES: O rare Hippias, will you be so good as not to laugh, if I find a difficulty in following you, and repeat my questions several times over? Please to answer me kindly and gently.

HIPPIAS: I should be greatly ashamed of myself, Socrates, if I, who teach others and take money of them, could not, when I was asked by you, answer in a civil and agreeable manner.

SOCRATES: Thank you: the fact is, that I seemed to understand what you meant when you said that the poet intended Achilles to be the bravest of men, and also that he intended Nestor to be the wisest; but when you said that he meant Odysseus to be the wiliest, I must confess that I could not understand what you were saying. Will you tell me, and then I shall perhaps understand you better; has not Homer made Achilles wily?

HIPPIAS: Certainly not, Socrates; he is the most straight-forward of mankind, and when Homer introduces them talking with one another in the passage called the Prayers, Achilles is supposed by the poet to say to Odysseus:—

'Son of Laertes, sprung from heaven, crafty Odysseus, I will speak out plainly the word which I intend to carry out in act, and which will, I believe, be accomplished. For I hate him like the gates of death who thinks one thing and says another. But I will speak that which shall be accomplished.'

Now, in these verses he clearly indicates the character of the two men; he shows Achilles to be true and simple, and Odysseus to be wily and false; for he supposes Achilles to be addressing Odysseus in these lines.

SOCRATES: Now, Hippias, I think that I understand your meaning; when you say that Odysseus is wily, you clearly mean that he is false?

HIPPIAS: Exactly so, Socrates; it is the character of Odysseus, as he is represented by Homer in many passages both of the Iliad and Odyssey.

SOCRATES: And Homer must be presumed to have meant that the true man is not the same as the false?

HIPPIAS: Of course, Socrates.

SOCRATES: And is that your own opinion, Hippias?

HIPPIAS: Certainly; how can I have any other?

SOCRATES: Well, then, as there is no possibility of asking Homer what he meant in these verses of his, let us leave him; but as you show a willingness to take up his cause, and your opinion agrees with what you declare to be his, will you answer on behalf of yourself and him?

HIPPIAS: I will; ask shortly anything which you like.

SOCRATES: Do you say that the false, like the sick, have no power to do things, or that they have the power to do things?

HIPPIAS: I should say that they have power to do many things, and in particular to deceive mankind.

SOCRATES: Then, according to you, they are both powerful and wily, are they not?

HIPPIAS: Yes.

SOCRATES: And are they wily, and do they deceive by reason of their simplicity and folly, or by reason of their cunning and a certain sort of prudence?

HIPPIAS: By reason of their cunning and prudence, most certainly.

SOCRATES: Then they are prudent, I suppose?

HIPPIAS: So they are—very.

SOCRATES: And if they are prudent, do they know or do they not know what they do?

HIPPIAS: Of course, they know very well; and that is why they do mischief to others.

SOCRATES: And having this knowledge, are they ignorant, or are they wise?

HIPPIAS: Wise, certainly; at least, in so far as they can deceive.

SOCRATES: Stop, and let us recall to mind what

you are saying; are you not saying that the false are powerful and prudent and knowing and wise in those things about which they are false?

HIPPIAS: To be sure.

SOCRATES: And the true differ from the false—the true and the false are the very opposite of each other?

HIPPIAS: That is my view.

SOCRATES: Then, according to your view, it would seem that the false are to be ranked in the class of the powerful and wise?

HIPPIAS: Assuredly.

SOCRATES: And when you say that the false are powerful and wise in so far as they are false, do you mean that they have or have not the power of uttering their falsehoods if they like?

HIPPIAS: I mean to say that they have the power.

SOCRATES: In a word, then, the false are they who are wise and have the power to speak falsely?

HIPPIAS: Yes.

SOCRATES: Then a man who has not the power of speaking falsely and is ignorant cannot be false?

HIPPIAS: You are right.

SOCRATES: And every man has power who does that which he wishes at the time when he wishes. I am not speaking of any special case in which he is prevented by disease or something of that sort, but I am speaking generally, as I might say of you, that you are able to write my name when you like. Would you not call a man able who could do that?

HIPPIAS: Yes.

SOCRATES: And tell me, Hippias, are you not a skilful calculator and arithmetician?

HIPPIAS: Yes, Socrates, assuredly I am.

SOCRATES: And if some one were to ask you what is the sum of 3 multiplied by 700, you would tell him the true answer in a moment, if you pleased?

HIPPIAS: certainly I should.

SOCRATES: Is not that because you are the wisest and ablest of men in these matters?

HIPPIAS: Yes.

SOCRATES: And being as you are the wisest and ablest of men in these matters of calculation, are you not also the best?

HIPPIAS: To be sure, Socrates, I am the best.

SOCRATES: And therefore you would be the most able to tell the truth about these matters, would you not?

HIPPIAS: Yes, I should.

SOCRATES: And could you speak falsehoods about them equally well? I must beg, Hippias, that you will answer me with the same frankness and magnanimity which has hitherto characterized you. If a person were to ask you what is the sum of 3 multiplied by 700, would not you be the best and most consistent teller of a falsehood, having always the power of speaking falsely as you have of speaking truly, about these same matters, if you wanted to tell a falsehood, and not to answer truly? Would the ignorant man be better able to tell a falsehood in matters of calculation than you would be, if you chose? Might he not sometimes stumble upon the truth, when he wanted to tell a lie, because he did not know, whereas you who are the wise man, if you wanted to tell a lie would always and consistently lie?

HIPPIAS: Yes, there you are quite right.

SOCRATES: Does the false man tell lies about other things, but not about number, or when he is making a calculation?

HIPPIAS: To be sure; he would tell as many lies about number as about other things.

SOCRATES: Then may we further assume, Hippias, that there are men who are false about calculation and number?

HIPPIAS: Yes.

SOCRATES: Who can they be? For you have already admitted that he who is false must have the ability to be false: you said, as you will remember, that he who is unable to be false will not be false?

HIPPIAS: Yes, I remember; it was so said.

SOCRATES: And were you not yourself just now shown to be best able to speak falsely about calculation?

HIPPIAS: Yes; that was another thing which was said.

SOCRATES: And are you not likewise said to speak truly about calculation?

HIPPIAS: Certainly.

SOCRATES: Then the same person is able to speak both falsely and truly about calculation? And that person is he who is good at calculation—the arithmetician?

HIPPIAS: Yes.

SOCRATES: Who, then, Hippias, is discovered to be false at calculation? Is he not the good man? For the good man is the able man, and he is the true man.

HIPPIAS: That is evident.

SOCRATES: Do you not see, then, that the same man is false and also true about the same matters? And the true man is not a whit better than the false; for indeed he is the same with him and not the very opposite, as you were just now imagining.

HIPPIAS: Not in that instance, clearly.

SOCRATES: Shall we examine other instances?

HIPPIAS: Certainly, if you are disposed.

SOCRATES: Are you not also skilled in geometry?

HIPPIAS: I am.

SOCRATES: Well, and does not the same hold in that science also? Is not the same person best able to speak falsely or to speak truly about diagrams; and he is —the geometrician?

HIPPIAS: Yes.

SOCRATES: He and no one else is good at it?

HIPPIAS: Yes, he and no one else.

SOCRATES: Then the good and wise geometer has this double power in the highest degree; and if there be a man who is false about diagrams the good man will be he, for he is able to be false; whereas the bad is unable, and for this reason is not false, as has been admitted.

HIPPIAS: True.

SOCRATES: Once more—let us examine a third case; that of the astronomer, in whose art, again, you, Hippias, profess to be a still greater proficient than in the preceding—do you not?

HIPPIAS: Yes, I am.

SOCRATES: And does not the same hold of astronomy?

HIPPIAS: True, Socrates.

SOCRATES: And in astronomy, too, if any man be

able to speak falsely he will be the good astronomer, but he who is not able will not speak falsely, for he has no knowledge.

HIPPIAS: Clearly not.

SOCRATES: Then in astronomy also, the same man will be true and false?

HIPPIAS: It would seem so.

SOCRATES: And now, Hippias, consider the question at large about all the sciences, and see whether the same principle does not always hold. I know that in most arts you are the wisest of men, as I have heard you boasting in the agora at the tables of the money-changers, when you were setting forth the great and enviable stores of your wisdom; and you said that upon one occasion, when you went to the Olympic games, all that you had on your person was made by yourself. You began with your ring, which was of your own workmanship, and you said that you could engrave rings; and you had another seal which was also of your own workmanship, and a strigil and an oil flask, which you had made yourself; you said also that you had made the shoes which you had on your feet, and the cloak and the short tunic; but what appeared to us all most extraordinary and a proof of singular art, was the girdle of your tunic, which, you said, was as fine as the most costly Persian fabric, and of your own weaving;

moreover, you told us that you had brought with you poems, epic, tragic, and dithyrambic, as well as prose writings of the most various kinds; and you said that your skill was also pre-eminent in the arts which I was just now mentioning, and in the true principles of rhythm and harmony and of orthography; and if I remember rightly, there were a great many other accomplishments in which you excelled. I have forgotten to mention your art of memory, which you regard as your special glory, and I dare say that I have forgotten many other things; but, as I was saying, only look to your own arts—and there are plenty of them— and to those of others; and tell me, having regard to the admissions which you and I have made, whether you discover any department of art or any description of wisdom or cunning, whichever name you use, in which the true and false are different and not the same: tell me, if you can, of any. But you cannot.

HIPPIAS: Not without consideration, Socrates.

SOCRATES: Nor will consideration help you, Hippias, as I believe; but then if I am right, remember what the consequence will be.

HIPPIAS: I do not know what you mean, Socrates.

SOCRATES: I suppose that you are not using your art of memory, doubtless because you think that such an accomplishment is not needed on the present occasion. I will therefore remind you of what you were saying: were you not saying that Achilles was a true man, and Odysseus false and wily?

HIPPIAS: I was.

SOCRATES: And now do you perceive that the same person has turned out to be false as well as true? If Odysseus is false he is also true, and if Achilles is true he is also false, and so the two men are not opposed to one another, but they are alike.

HIPPIAS: O Socrates, you are always weaving the meshes of an argument, selecting the most difficult point, and fastening upon details instead of grappling with the matter in hand as a whole. Come now, and I will demonstrate to you, if you will allow me, by many satisfactory proofs, that Homer has made Achilles a better man than Odysseus, and a truthful man too; and that he has made the other crafty, and a teller of many untruths, and inferior to Achilles. And then, if you please, you shall make a speech on the other side, in order to prove that Odysseus is the better man; and this may be compared to mine, and then the company will know which of us is the better speaker.

SOCRATES: O Hippias, I do not doubt that you are wiser than I am. But I have a way, when anybody else says anything, of giving close attention to him, especially if the speaker appears to me to be a wise man. Having a desire to understand, I question him, and I examine and analyse and put together what he says, in order that I may understand; but if the speaker appears to me to be a poor hand, I do not interrogate him, or trouble myself about him, and you may know by this who they are whom I deem to be wise men, for you will see that when I am talking with a wise man, I am very attentive to what he says; and I ask questions of him, in order that I may learn, and be improved by him. And I could not help remarking while you were speaking, that when you recited the verses in which Achilles, as you argued, attacks Odysseus as a deceiver, that you must be strangely mistaken, because Odysseus, the man of wiles, is never found to tell a lie; but Achilles is found to be wily on your own showing. At any rate he speaks falsely; for first he utters these words, which you just now repeated,—

'He is hateful to me even as the gates of death who thinks one thing and says another:'—

And then he says, a little while afterwards, he will not be persuaded by Odysseus and Agamemnon, neither will he remain at Troy; but, says he,—

'To-morrow, when I have offered sacrifices to Zeus and all the Gods, having loaded my ships well, I will drag them down into the deep; and then you shall see, if you have a mind, and if such things are a care to you, early in the morning my ships sailing over the fishy Hellespont, and my men eagerly plying the oar; and, if the illustrious shaker of the earth gives me a good voyage, on the third day I shall reach the fertile Phthia.'

And before that, when he was reviling Agamemnon, he said,—

'And now to Phthia I will go, since to return home in the beaked ships is far better, nor am I inclined to stay here in dishonour and amass wealth and riches for you.'

But although on that occasion, in the presence of the whole army, he spoke after this fashion, and on the other occasion to his companions, he appears never to have made any preparation or attempt to draw down the ships, as if he had the least intention of sailing home; so nobly regardless was he of the truth. Now I, Hippias, originally asked you the question, because I was in doubt as to which of the two heroes was intended by the poet to be the best, and because I thought that both of them were the best, and that it would be difficult to decide which was the better of them, not only in respect of truth and falsehood, but of virtue generally, for even in this matter of speaking the truth they are much upon a par.

HIPPIAS: There you are wrong, Socrates; for in so far as Achilles speaks falsely, the falsehood is obviously unintentional. He is compelled against his will to remain and rescue the army in their misfortune. But when Odysseus speaks falsely he is voluntarily and intentionally false.

SOCRATES: You, sweet Hippias, like Odysseus, are a deceiver yourself.

HIPPIAS: Certainly not, Socrates; what makes you say so?

SOCRATES: Because you say that Achilles does not speak falsely from design, when he is not only a deceiver, but besides being a braggart, in Homer's description of him is so cunning, and so far superior to Odysseus in lying and pretending, that he dares to contradict himself, and Odysseus does not find him out; at any rate he does not appear to say anything to him which would imply that he perceived his falsehood.

HIPPIAS: What do you mean, Socrates?

SOCRATES: Did you not observe that afterwards, when he is speaking to Odysseus, he says that he will sail away with the early dawn; but to Ajax he tells quite a different story?

HIPPIAS: Where is that?

SOCRATES: Where he says,—

'I will not think about bloody war until the son of warlike Priam, illustrious Hector, comes to the tents and ships of the Myrmidons, slaughtering the Argives, and burning the ships with fire; and about my tent and dark ship, I suspect that Hector, although eager for the battle, will nevertheless stay his hand.'

Now, do you really think, Hippias, that the son of Thetis, who had been the pupil of the sage Cheiron, had such a bad memory, or would have carried the art of lying to such an extent (when he had been assailing liars in the most violent terms only the instant before) as to say to Odysseus that he would sail away, and to Ajax that he would remain, and that he was not rather practising upon the simplicity of Odysseus, whom he regarded as an ancient, and thinking that he would get the better of him by his own cunning and falsehood?

HIPPIAS: No, I do not agree with you, Socrates; but I believe that Achilles is induced to say one thing to Ajax, and another to Odysseus in the innocence of his heart, whereas Odysseus, whether he speaks falsely or truly, speaks always with a purpose.

SOCRATES: Then Odysseus would appear after all to be better than Achilles?

HIPPIAS: Certainly not, Socrates.

SOCRATES: Why, were not the voluntary liars only just now shown to be better than the involuntary?

HIPPIAS: And how, Socrates, can those who intentionally err, and voluntarily and designedly commit iniquities, be better than those who err and do wrong involuntarily? Surely there is a great excuse to be made for a man telling a falsehood, or doing an injury or any sort of harm to another in ignorance. And the laws are obviously far more severe on those who lie or do evil, voluntarily, than on those who do evil involuntarily.

SOCRATES: You see, Hippias, as I have already told you, how pertinacious I am in asking questions of wise men. And I think that this is the only good point about me, for I am full of defects, and always getting wrong in some way or other. My deficiency is proved to me by the fact that when I meet one of you who are famous for wisdom, and to whose wisdom all the Hellenes are witnesses, I am found out to know nothing. For speaking generally, I hardly ever have the same opinion about anything which you have, and what proof of ignorance can be greater than to differ from wise men? But I have one singular good quality, which is my salvation; I am not ashamed to learn, and I ask and enquire, and am very grateful to those who answer me, and never fail to give them my grateful thanks; and when I learn a thing I never deny my teacher, or pretend that the lesson is a discovery of my own; but I praise his wisdom, and proclaim what I have learned from him. And now I cannot agree in what you are saying, but I strongly disagree. Well, I know that this is my own fault, and is a defect in my character, but I will not pretend to be more than I am; and my opinion, Hippias, is the very contrary of what you are saying. For I maintain that those who hurt or injure mankind, and speak falsely and deceive, and err voluntarily, are better far than those who do wrong involuntarily. Sometimes, however, I am of the opposite opinion; for I am all abroad in my ideas about this matter, a condition obviously occasioned by ignorance. And just now I happen to be in a crisis of my disorder at which those who err voluntarily appear to me better than those who err involuntarily. My present state of mind is due to our previous argument, which inclines me to believe that in general those who do wrong involuntarily are worse than those who do wrong voluntarily, and therefore I hope that you will be good to me, and not refuse to heal me; for you will do me a much greater benefit if you cure my soul of ignorance, than you would if you were to cure my body of disease. I must, however, tell you beforehand, that if you make a long oration to me you will not cure me, for I shall not be able to follow you; but if you will answer me, as you did just now, you will do me a great deal of good, and I do not think that you will be any the worse yourself. And I have some claim upon you also, O son of Apemantus, for you incited me to converse with

Hippias; and now, if Hippias will not answer me, you must entreat him on my behalf.

EUDICUS: But I do not think, Socrates, that Hippias will require any entreaty of mine; for he has already said that he will refuse to answer no man.—Did you not say so, Hippias?

HIPPIAS: Yes, I did; but then, Eudicus, Socrates is always troublesome in an argument, and appears to be dishonest. (Compare Gorgias; Republic.)

SOCRATES: Excellent Hippias, I do not do so intentionally (if I did, it would show me to be a wise man and a master of wiles, as you would argue), but unintentionally, and therefore you must pardon me; for, as you say, he who is unintentionally dishonest should be pardoned.

EUDICUS: Yes, Hippias, do as he says; and for our sake, and also that you may not belie your profession, answer whatever Socrates asks you.

HIPPIAS: I will answer, as you request me; and do you ask whatever you like.

SOCRATES: I am very desirous, Hippias, of examining this question, as to which are the better—those who err voluntarily or involuntarily? And if you will answer me, I think that I can put you in the way of approaching the subject: You would admit, would you not, that there are good runners?

HIPPIAS: Yes.

SOCRATES: And there are bad runners?

HIPPIAS: Yes.

SOCRATES: And he who runs well is a good runner, and he who runs ill is a bad runner?

HIPPIAS: Very true.

SOCRATES: And he who runs slowly runs ill, and he who runs quickly runs well?

HIPPIAS: Yes.

SOCRATES: Then in a race, and in running, swiftness is a good, and slowness is an evil quality?

HIPPIAS: To be sure.

SOCRATES: Which of the two then is a better runner? He who runs slowly voluntarily, or he who runs slowly involuntarily?

HIPPIAS: He who runs slowly voluntarily.

SOCRATES: And is not running a species of doing?

HIPPIAS: Certainly.

SOCRATES: And if a species of doing, a species of action?

HIPPIAS: Yes.

SOCRATES: Then he who runs badly does a bad and dishonourable action in a race?

HIPPIAS: Yes; a bad action, certainly.

SOCRATES: And he who runs slowly runs badly?

HIPPIAS: Yes.

SOCRATES: Then the good runner does this bad and disgraceful action voluntarily, and the bad involuntarily?

HIPPIAS: That is to be inferred.

SOCRATES: Then he who involuntarily does evil actions, is worse in a race than he who does them voluntarily?

HIPPIAS: Yes, in a race.

SOCRATES: Well, but at a wrestling match—which is the better wrestler, he who falls voluntarily or involuntarily?

HIPPIAS: He who falls voluntarily, doubtless.

SOCRATES: And is it worse or more dishonourable at a wrestling match, to fall, or to throw another?

HIPPIAS: To fall.

SOCRATES: Then, at a wrestling match, he who voluntarily does base and dishonourable actions is a better wrestler than he who does them involuntarily?

HIPPIAS: That appears to be the truth.

SOCRATES: And what would you say of any other bodily exercise—is not he who is better made able to do both that which is strong and that which is weak—that which is fair and that which is foul?—so that when he does bad actions with the body, he who is better made does them voluntarily, and he who is worse made does them involuntarily.

HIPPIAS: Yes, that appears to be true about strength.

SOCRATES: And what do you say about grace, Hippias? Is not he who is better made able to assume evil and disgraceful figures and postures voluntarily, as he who is worse made assumes them involuntarily?

HIPPIAS: True.

SOCRATES: Then voluntary ungracefulness comes from excellence of the bodily frame, and involuntary from the defect of the bodily frame?

HIPPIAS: True.

SOCRATES: And what would you say of an unmusical voice; would you prefer the voice which is voluntarily or involuntarily out of tune?

HIPPIAS: That which is voluntarily out of tune.

SOCRATES: The involuntary is the worse of the two?

HIPPIAS: Yes.

SOCRATES: And would you choose to possess goods or evils?

HIPPIAS: Goods.

SOCRATES: And would you rather have feet which are voluntarily or involuntarily lame?

HIPPIAS: Feet which are voluntarily lame.

SOCRATES: But is not lameness a defect or deformity?

HIPPIAS: Yes.

SOCRATES: And is not blinking a defect in the eyes?

HIPPIAS: Yes.

SOCRATES: And would you rather always have eyes with which you might voluntarily blink and not see, or with which you might involuntarily blink?

HIPPIAS: I would rather have eyes which voluntarily blink.

SOCRATES: Then in your own case you deem that which voluntarily acts ill, better than that which involuntarily acts ill?

HIPPIAS: Yes, certainly, in cases such as you mention.

SOCRATES: And does not the same hold of ears, nostrils, mouth, and of all the senses—those which involuntarily act ill are not to be desired, as being defective; and those which voluntarily act ill are to be desired as being good?

HIPPIAS: I agree.

SOCRATES: And what would you say of instruments;—which are the better sort of instruments to have to do with?—those with which a man acts ill voluntarily or involuntarily? For example, had a man better have a rudder with which he will steer ill, voluntarily or involuntarily?

HIPPIAS: He had better have a rudder with which he will steer ill voluntarily.

SOCRATES: And does not the same hold of the bow and the lyre, the flute and all other things?

HIPPIAS: Very true.

SOCRATES: And would you rather have a horse of such a temper that you may ride him ill voluntarily or involuntarily?

HIPPIAS: I would rather have a horse which I could ride ill voluntarily.

SOCRATES: That would be the better horse?

HIPPIAS: Yes.

SOCRATES: Then with a horse of better temper, vicious actions would be produced voluntarily; and with a horse of bad temper involuntarily?

HIPPIAS: Certainly.

SOCRATES: And that would be true of a dog, or of any other animal?

HIPPIAS: Yes.

SOCRATES: And is it better to possess the mind of an archer who voluntarily or involuntarily misses the mark?

HIPPIAS: Of him who voluntarily misses.

SOCRATES: This would be the better mind for the purposes of archery?

HIPPIAS: Yes.

SOCRATES: Then the mind which involuntarily errs is worse than the mind which errs voluntarily?

HIPPIAS: Yes, certainly, in the use of the bow.

SOCRATES: And what would you say of the art of medicine;—has not the mind which voluntarily works harm to the body, more of the healing art?

HIPPIAS: Yes.

SOCRATES: Then in the art of medicine the voluntary is better than the involuntary?

HIPPIAS: Yes.

SOCRATES: Well, and in lute-playing and in flute-playing, and in all arts and sciences, is not that mind the better which voluntarily does what is evil and dishonourable, and goes wrong, and is not the worse that which does so involuntarily?

HIPPIAS: That is evident.

SOCRATES: And what would you say of the characters of slaves? Should we not prefer to have those who voluntarily do wrong and make mistakes, and are they not better in their mistakes than those who commit them involuntarily?

HIPPIAS: Yes.

SOCRATES: And should we not desire to have our own minds in the best state possible?

HIPPIAS: Yes.

SOCRATES: And will our minds be better if they do wrong and make mistakes voluntarily or involuntarily?

HIPPIAS: O, Socrates, it would be a monstrous thing to say that those who do wrong voluntarily are better than those who do wrong involuntarily!

SOCRATES: And yet that appears to be the only inference.

HIPPIAS: I do not think so.

SOCRATES: But I imagined, Hippias, that you did. Please to answer once more: Is not justice a power, or knowledge, or both? Must not justice, at all events, be one of these?

HIPPIAS: Yes.

SOCRATES: But if justice is a power of the soul, then the soul which has the greater power is also the more just; for that which has the greater power, my good friend, has been proved by us to be the better.

HIPPIAS: Yes, that has been proved.

SOCRATES: And if justice is knowledge, then the wiser will be the juster soul, and the more ignorant the more unjust?

HIPPIAS: Yes.

SOCRATES: But if justice be power as well as knowledge—then will not the soul which has both knowledge and power be the more just, and that which is the more ignorant be the more unjust? Must it not be so?

HIPPIAS: Clearly.

SOCRATES: And is not the soul which has the greater power and wisdom also better, and better able to do both good and evil in every action?

HIPPIAS: Certainly.

SOCRATES: The soul, then, which acts ill, acts voluntarily by power and art—and these either one or both of them are elements of justice?

HIPPIAS: That seems to be true.

SOCRATES: And to do injustice is to do ill, and not to do injustice is to do well?

HIPPIAS: Yes.

SOCRATES: And will not the better and abler soul when it does wrong, do wrong voluntarily, and the bad soul involuntarily?

HIPPIAS: Clearly.

SOCRATES: And the good man is he who has the good soul, and the bad man is he who has the bad?

HIPPIAS: Yes.

SOCRATES: Then the good man will voluntarily

do wrong, and the bad man involuntarily, if the good man is he who has the good soul?

HIPPIAS: Which he certainly has.

SOCRATES: Then, Hippias, he who voluntarily does wrong and disgraceful things, if there be such a man, will be the good man?

HIPPIAS: There I cannot agree with you.

SOCRATES: Nor can I agree with myself, Hippias; and yet that seems to be the conclusion which, as far as we can see at present, must follow from our argument. As I was saying before, I am all abroad, and being in perplexity am always changing my opinion. Now, that I or any ordinary man should wander in perplexity is not surprising; but if you wise men also wander, and we cannot come to you and rest from our wandering, the matter begins to be serious both to us and to you.

Made in United States
North Haven, CT
11 September 2024

57246164R00024